LADY WALLACE (S 32), BY CHARLES-AUGUSTE LEBOURG (1872)
(Founders' Room)

WALLACE COLLECTION CATALOGUES

A SHORT ILLUSTRATED
HISTORY OF THE
WALLACE COLLECTION
AND ITS FOUNDERS

BY
TRENCHARD COX, M.A.

LONDON: PRINTED FOR THE TRUSTEES OF THE WALLACE
COLLECTION AND SOLD AT HERTFORD HOUSE
PRICE ONE SHILLING
1936

2854

PRINTED IN GREAT BRITAIN BY
WILLIAM CLOWES AND SONS, LTD.,
LONDON AND BECCLES.

CONTENTS

ADMINISTRATION

BOARD OF TRUSTEES

STAFF

Keeper and Inspector of the Armouries—
James G. Mann, M.A., B.Litt., F.S.A.
Assistant to the Keeper and Lecturer—W. P. Gibson, B.A.
Assistant to the Keeper—Trenchard Cox, M.A.

The Keeper invites communications from visitors able to supply fresh information about any object in the Collection. All letters should be addressed—The Keeper, Wallace Collection, Manchester Square, W.1.

ADMISSION

THE WALLACE COLLECTION is open on WEEK-DAYS from 10 a.m. to 5 p.m., and on SUNDAYS from 2 to 5 p.m.

ADMISSION FREE on Sundays, Mondays, Wednesdays, Thursdays and Saturdays ; SIXPENCE on Tuesdays and Fridays.

Closed on Good Friday, Christmas Eve and Christmas Day.

CATALOGUES

The following Official Catalogues are sold only at Hertford House. They can be obtained through the post upon application to the Keeper. A remittance should accompany the application :—

1—Pictures and Drawings (Illustrated Text)	3s. 6d.,	postage 9d.
Bound in buff linen	5s. 0d.	,, 9d.
2—Pictures and Drawings (Illustrations)	2s. 6d.	,, 6d.
Bound in buff linen	3s. 6d.	,, 6d.
3—Objects of Art (Illustrations)	2s. 6d.	,, 6d.
Bound in buff linen	5s. 0d.	,, 6d.
4—European Arms and Armour (Illustrated). Part I .	2s. 0d.	,, 6d.
Bound in buff linen	3s. 6d.	,, 6d.
5—European Arms and Armour (Illustrated). Part II .	2s. 6d.	,, 6d.
Bound in buff linen	5s. 0d.	,, 6d.
6—European Arms and Armour (Illustrated). Part III. (In preparation.)		
7—Catalogue of Sculpture	3s. 6d.	,, 6d.
Bound in buff linen	5s. 0d.	,, 6d.
8—Three Lectures upon French Painting . . .	6d.	,, 2d.
9—General Guide	1s. 0d.	,, 6d.
Bound in buff linen	2s. 0d.	,, 6d.
10—Catalogue of Miniatures	2s. 6d.	,, 6d.
Bound in blue buckram	3s. 6d.	,, 6d.
11—A Short Illustrated History of the Wallace Collection and its Founders	1s. 0d.	,, 6d.

PHOTOGRAPHS

Photographs of a large number of the pictures and objects of art are on sale at the Catalogue Stall at prices ranging from 1s. to 2s. 6d. The prints are copyright and a fee of 5s. is charged for permission to reproduce. Order forms and a list of objects already photographed can be sent on application.

POSTCARDS

Sepia postcards of about 300 pictures and objects of art are on sale at 1d. each. (Size 5½ in. by 3½ in.)

COLOURED POSTCARDS

Postcards in colour of a limited number of the pictures are obtainable, price 2d. each, postage 1d. for six. (Size 5⅞ in. by 4⅛ in.) These cards, framed in *passe-partout* for standing or hanging-up, are on sale at 6d. each. *They cannot be sent through the post.*

CHRISTMAS CARDS

Slip-in mounts for framing coloured postcards of the vertical pictures, printed with Christmas and New Year Greetings, are on sale, price 3d. (plain envelope included). They are supplied in various tints : ivory, light buff, silver-grey, blue and dull grey.

COLOURED PRINTS

A limited number of the pictures have been reproduced in chromo-collotype. The prints measure about 10 in. by 8 in., on a mount of 17 in. by 14 in. Price 2s. 6d. Portfolio, 3s. 6d.

They can be forwarded through the post on the payment of the postage (single prints, 3½d., plus ½d. for each additional print) and packing (3d. for a carton that will contain six prints). Coloured prints, framed like the cards in *passe-partout*, are on sale at 3s. 6d.

Cheques and Money Orders should be made payable to *The Keeper* and crossed *H.M. Paymaster-General, Account Wallace Collection.* No order can be executed until a remittance has been received.

LECTURES

The free Lectures form a course which covers the whole Collection and is repeated with variations every month. Each lecture, however, is complete in itself. The lectures are varied by changes in the aspect from which the subjects are considered and in the choice of objects to illustrate them. A syllabus of the lectures to be delivered every month can be obtained at the Catalogue Stall or by application to the Keeper. The lectures are given on Saturdays at 12 noon, and on all other week-days (Wednesdays excepted) at 3 p.m.

The services of the Lecturer can also be secured for Private Parties. Application should be made to the Keeper at least seven days in advance. A charge of 15s. 0d. (payable at the Catalogue Stall before the lecture) will be made for each party.

FIRST FLOOR

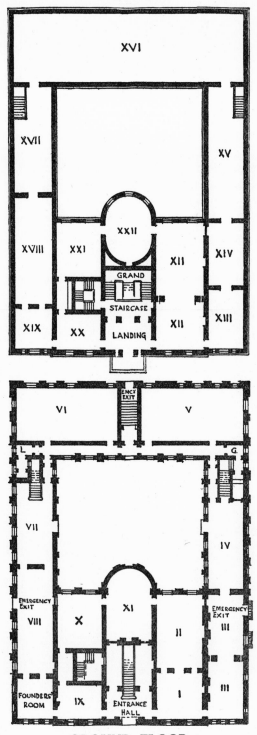

GROUND FLOOR

PLANS OF THE GALLERIES AT THE PRESENT TIME

KEY TO PLANS OF THE GALLERIES AT THE PRESENT TIME

GROUND FLOOR

ENTRANCE HALL—Stall for the sale of publications

    I—Portraits, Objects and Miniatures connected with the Royal House of France

    II—French and Dutch pictures, French furniture and Sèvres porcelain, astronomical clock

    III—Italian Renaissance bronzes, ivories, wood-carvings, plaquettes and majolica. Pages from illuminated books

    IV—Wax Reliefs and Oriental Armour

V–VII—European Arms and Armour

    VIII—French Sculpture and Renaissance Furniture

FOUNDERS' ROOM—Portraits and Busts of the Hertford family

    IX—Portraits of historical interest connected with the Royal House of England

PASSAGE—Watercolours

    X—Pictures of the Dutch and Flemish Schools : Boulle Furniture ; Goldsmiths' work

    XI—Miniatures, and paintings by J. B. Oudry

ARRANGEMENT IN THE TIME OF SIR RICHARD WALLACE

I—Front State Room   II—Back State Room

III—(Front) Canaletto Room   IV—Smoking Room

    (Back) Sixteenth-Century Room   VIII—Butler's Quarters

V, VI, VII—Coach-house, Stable-yard, Stables

FOUNDERS' ROOM—Housekeeper's Room

    IX—Breakfast Room   X—Billiard Room

                               XI—Dining Room

KEY TO PLANS OF THE GALLERIES AT THE PRESENT TIME

FIRST FLOOR

GRAND STAIRCASE—Pictures by Boucher ; busts by Houdon and Coysevox

XII—Pictures by Canaletto and Guardi : Sèvres Porcelain

XIII–XIV—Dutch and Flemish Schools, seventeenth century

XV—French and British Schools, nineteenth century

XVI—The Long Picture Gallery. Contains paintings by Titian, Rubens, Van Dyck, De Hooch, Rembrandt, Hals, Gainsborough and Reynolds, as well as outstanding examples of French Furniture

XVII—Italian and Flemish Pictures of the Renaissance

XVIII—Pictures by Watteau, Lancret, Pater, Fragonard and Greuze ; French Furniture of the late eighteenth century ; Snuff-boxes

XIX—Pictures by Boucher, Watteau and Greuze ; French Furniture of the late eighteenth century

PASSAGE—Sketches by Bonington ; Sèvres Porcelain

XX–XXII—French Pictures, Furniture and Porcelain of the eighteenth century

ARRANGEMENT IN THE TIME OF SIR RICHARD WALLACE

XII—(Front) Small Drawing Room (Back) Large Drawing Room

XIII—East Drawing Room

XIV—Oriental Armoury

XV—Modern Picture Gallery

XVI—Large Gallery ; North Picture Gallery

XVII—European Armoury

XVIII—Dressing-Rooms and Bath-Room

XIX—Lady Wallace's Bedroom

XX—Boudoir

XXI—Study

XXII—Oval Drawing Room

PREFACE

THIS book was prepared under the supervision of my predecessor, the late Mr. S. J. Camp, F.S.A. He had been associated with the Collection since it was first opened to the public in 1900, and had seen it grow from a Nine Days' Wonder when 19,269 people thronged inside its doors in the first week, to become one of the accepted institutions of London. When Lord Salisbury's Government purchased the freehold of Hertford House it insured that the Collection would remain in the setting in which it had been assembled by its last owners. Conditions have changed much in the last forty years, and many of the great town houses of London have been demolished. This gives an added interest to the series of photographs, now published for the first time, and to the folding plans at the end, which show the interior of Hertford House as it was during private occupation. In his later years Sir Richard Wallace entertained little, and there are few alive to-day who knew him personally. Mr. Camp felt that the time had come to collect and set down all that could still be learned before it was too late. It is hoped that the public who visit the Collection may be interested to know something of its origins and of the personalities of three generations concerned in its formation.

JAMES G. MANN,
Keeper

July, 1936

INTRODUCTION

THE primary object in producing this book was to publish a selection from a set of 57 photographs of Hertford House, which were taken before it was converted into a public museum. They have, among their other claims to interest, that of illustrating the method—widely different from our own to-day—of hanging pictures and arranging furniture some 45 years ago. As the scheme for the book took more definite shape, it seemed worth while to include other photographs of persons, places and objects connected with the formation of the Collection, and to preface them by a short historical introduction.

Much of the information given in the text has been taken from the introduction to the *Catalogue of Pictures and Drawings in the Wallace Collection* (1928), and certain sections are reprinted from the *General Guide* (1933). My acknowledgments are due to officials of the British Museum, the Bibliothèque Nationale and the Musée Carnavalet, Paris, the editors of *l'Illustration*, and the Director of the Cimetière de l'Est, for their permission to reproduce certain photographs ; and to Miss Alicia Scott, sister of the late Sir John Murray Scott. I have to thank Mr. James G. Mann, F.S.A., recently appointed Keeper, for having put at my disposal the result of personal researches, and Mr. William Gibson, Assistant to the Keeper, for many valuable suggestions and for his help in seeing this small volume through the Press. Above all, I have been indebted to the late Keeper, Mr. S. J. Camp, who watched the progress of this book until within a few days of his death.

TRENCHARD COX

THE FOUNDERS

A SPIRIT of collecting and a sympathy with things French were present in the Hertford line long before Richard Seymour-Conway, the fourth Marquess (1800–1870), began to furnish his Paris home with masterpieces of French art. Indeed his remote ancestor, of the sixteenth century, Edward Seymour (1506–1552), brother to Queen Jane Seymour, the first Earl of Hertford, first Duke of Somerset, Lord Protector of England and Governor of the young King Edward VI (1547), was a man of high intellectual distinction. He lived in close association with France, and employed a cultivated French nobleman as tutor to his daughters who, themselves, produced a volume of poems in French extolling the virtues of Margaret of Navarre. A portrait (which formerly belonged to William Beckford of Fonthill), supposed to be of the first Earl, by Corneille de Lyon (*op. c.* 1530–1575) is in the collection.

Edward Seymour's persistent clemency, although a Protestant, towards the Roman Catholics brought him to the headsman's block ; and his titles and estates were entailed, by an Act of Parliament passed in 1540, upon his issue by his second wife, Anne Stanhope. The line became extinct in 1750 with Algernon Seymour, seventh Duke of Somerset.

THE FIRST MARQUESS

The Earldom of Hertford, however, was revived at once in the person of Francis Seymour-Conway (1719–1794), Second Baron Conway, a descendant of the Lord Protector's first marriage, who became, in 1793, the Earl of Yarmouth and the first Marquess of Hertford. (The Con-

way titles and estates had come to the family by marriage.)
The beginnings of our present collection were formed by
this nobleman, who also conformed to type by establishing
a connexion with the Continent through his appointment
as Ambassador to France from 1763–65. He was Lord-
Lieutenant of Ireland from 1765–66 and Lord Chamberlain from 1766 till 1782. A nephew of Sir Robert Walpole,
he married in 1741 Isabella, youngest daughter of Charles
second Duke of Grafton, and had seven sons and six
daughters. The *George III* by Allan Ramsay (No. 560),
now in Gallery IX, also the copies of Van Dyck's *Charles I*
and *Henrietta Maria* (Nos. 112 and 118) probably belonged
to the first Marquess ; whereas he certainly commis-
sioned Sir Joshua Reynolds to paint the portraits of two
of his daughters, the Ladies Elizabeth and Frances, for
which he paid £110. These and the two royal portraits
now hang in the Founders' Room (Nos. 31 and 33).

THE SECOND MARQUESS

The rather dim personality of the first holder of the
Hertford Marquisate found a contrast in his successor,
Francis Ingram Seymour-Conway (1743–1822). As Lord
Beauchamp he distinguished himself in the House of
Commons from 1766 to 1793, when he took the title of
Earl of Yarmouth upon his father being created a mar-
quess. His gifts and personality, and his freedom from
insularity of outlook caused him to be appointed Ambassador Extraordinary to Berlin and Vienna (1793–94).
He was Lord Chamberlain from 1812 to 1821. The second
Marquess's tastes in the arts were directed mainly to
contemporary English portraiture ; presumably he com-
missioned Downman to paint the portrait of his second
wife, which is dated 1781 and now hangs in the Founders'
Room (No. 754) ; he also probably acquired Reynolds'
portrait of Old " Q " (No. 561) ; and he laid two of the
corner-stones in the structure of the present collection of

English pictures by purchasing, in 1810, Romney's *Mrs.. Robinson* (in Gallery IX, No. 37) and Reynolds' *Nelly O'Brien* (Gallery XVI, No. 38), giving £21 for the first and £64 for the second.

Francis Ingram married twice. His first wife, Alice Eliza (*m.* 1768), was the daughter of the second Viscount Windsor. His second wife, Isabella Anne Ingram-Shepherd (*m.* 1776), a daughter of the tenth Viscount Irvine, added to the number of Seymours who came into close connexion with the Crown by succeeding Mrs. Fitzherbert in the affections of the Prince Regent, whose old yellow Berlin, in which the Prince liked to travel *incognito*, used often to rumble through Manchester Square. Indeed the Regent's visits to Manchester House gave much cause for tittle-tattle to contemporary busy-bodies, and were constant enough to become the subject of popular lampoons. A malicious verse in Tom Moore's diary runs :—

> Through M.nch.st.r. Squ.r. took a canter just now
> Met the Old Yellow Chariot and made a low bow.

Lady Hertford's interests were political as well as social ; she was a reactionary, a violent anti-catholic, and under her guidance Manchester House became a Tory meeting place. For about nine years (1811–20) she exercised considerable influence over the future George IV until, in 1820, she was forced to resign her position in favour of the plump and middle-aged Lady Conyngham who, in the parlance of popular gibing, became the Mistress Quickly to the King's Falstaff. A supposed miniature portrait of Lady Conyngham (M 306) is in Gallery XI (*see Catalogue of Miniatures*, p. 120).

THE THIRD MARQUESS

Isabella Hertford's only surviving child, Francis Charles Seymour-Conway (1777–1842), succeeded to the title as the third Marquess and, by the brilliance of his own accomplishments and by his spectacular mode of living, brought the house of Hertford into the foremost rank of fame and fashion. A portrait by Downman, now in the Founders' Room (No. 752), shows the Marquess when a child of five, and portrays his red hair, which later entitled him, when Earl of Yarmouth, to the nickname of "Red Herrings" or "Bloaters." The third Marquess had an adventurous life and cut a fine figure in political and court circles. From 1798, when he married the heiress Maria Fagnani, until his succession, he represented in turn the family boroughs of Oxford, Lisburn and Camelford in the House of Commons. In 1803 he was taken prisoner in France on landing at Calais immediately after the rupture of the Peace of Amiens, and was interned at Verdun for three years ; he was released in 1806 through Fox's negotiations with Napoleon and intercession with Talleyrand ; but his wife remained in France, where she is supposed, meanwhile, to have borne a child to her lover, Count Casimir de Montrond, the secretary of Talleyrand. In 1827 the Marquess was appointed as Envoy Extraordinary to the Court of Russia, whither he bore the Order of the Garter to Nicholas I, who was astonished by the personal magnificence of the English nobleman, more brilliant than that of any member of a Court which boasted of its semi-Asiatic splendours. At home the Marquess became the Court-Chamberlain and friend of the Prince Regent, whom he helped to form the collection of pictures—mainly Dutch—now at Buckingham Palace and Windsor Castle. The Marquess' wit and dissipation, combined with his lavish entertaining, made him a legendary personage in London, and both Thackeray and Disraeli introduced him as a character into their books. In *Vanity Fair* he appears as the Marquess of Steyne, a libertine whose town mansion, *Gaunt House*, concealed behind its forbidding portals his lordship's luxurious *petits appartements*, entered only by a modest back door by which, at late hours, closed carriages would come and go. In *Coningsby* Disraeli took him as a model

for Lord Monmouth. To these grim portrayals of fiction
one may, however, find a refreshing contrast of fact in(
the memoirs of Harriette Wilson, where she describes a
touching act of kindliness by Lord Hertford towards
her sister, Fanny, who, when she lay dying, asked for
some eau-de-Cologne to moisten her temples. Lord
Hertford, anxious to do anything that he " or his cook
could do useful for her," galloped from Brompton to
London and back in order to fetch the restorative. More-
over he ordered straw to be placed at Fanny's door, and
was the last man to take leave of her before she died,
touching her hand and saying, in a tone of real feeling,
" God bless you, poor thing."

By his marriage the third Marquess had intensified
the aura of romance which had encompassed him.
His wife was the heiress Maria (*Mie-Mie*), daughter
of Marchesa Fagnani, formerly an Italian dancer.
Although legally the daughter of the Marchese, rights
of paternity were claimed by two highly eccentric per-
sonages : George Selwyn of Matson, the wit of White's
and friend of Horace Walpole, and the Duke of Queens-
berry—*Old " Q,"* as famous a figure on the turf at New-
market (whither he once rode, for a wager, in a four-
wheeled machine " capable of travelling nineteen miles
an hour ") as he was in Piccadilly, where he was usually
to be seen sitting at the bow-window of No. 138, beneath
which he used to keep a mounted groom to carry amorous
missives to any likely passer-by. Both Selwyn and Queens-
berry left their disputed " daughter " great sums of money,
which, added to the means already owned by the third
Marquess, entailed a huge fortune to the Hertford family.
The Duke left the Marchioness £150,000, two houses in
Piccadilly and a villa at Richmond, which was only a
slender fraction of the amount left by the third Marquess,
who died possessed of nearly £2,000,000.

Although he inherited several houses, the third Marquess cared little for any residences other than Old

Dorchester House * (with ready access to Hyde Park, where the Marquess kept a cow), Manchester House, and St. Dunstan's lodge in Regent's Park, built for him by Decimus Burton (1800–1881). The last-named house (until recently the hospital for soldiers blinded in the Great War) bore on its façade the architectural clock with two life-size figures ("Striking Jacks"), which the Marquess bought (for £210) from the city church of St. Dunstan's-in-the-West, where it was put up, probably as a thankoffering by parishioners for the escape of the church from the Great Fire. A souvenir of childhood is said to have prompted Lord Hertford to buy the clock. As a child he was taken by his nurse to Fleet Street "if a good boy" to see the "old giants" strike the hours ; and he is said to have remarked that, when a man, he would possess the clock (much to the scepticism of his nurse, who would tell him that church clocks were not for sale). In 1829, however, the obstruction caused in Fleet Street by the crowds waiting to see the figures strike, as well as the imminent prospect of the church being demolished, prompted the authorities to have it removed—an action which caused Lord Hertford to purchase the clock and Charles Lamb to shed tears. In March 1935 the automaton clock, in company with three statues of King Lud and his sons (from Lud Gate), was replaced on the present church of St. Dunstan's-in-the-West, erected about 1833 on the site of the earlier church which was pulled down in 1830.

At St. Dunstan's, the third Marquess exploited the wide range of his interests by amassing a fine collection of bronzes, marbles and furniture, as well as an extensive library of Italian books. The pictures, however, were few, among them being the famous *Vision of S. Catherine* by Paul Veronese, now in the National Gallery (No. 1041). At Manchester House, on the other hand, paintings

* Old Dorchester House was demolished about 1850, to make way for Sir Robert Holford's Italianate mansion, begun in 1851.

played a larger part in the scheme of decoration, and there the third Marquess was able to indulge his taste for Dutch pictures, which were flooding the market at low prices as a result of the dispersion of many fine Dutch collections in the early years of the nineteenth century. Among the celebrated pictures which came into the Marquess' possession were *Perseus and Andromeda* by Titian (Gallery XVI, No. 11 ; bought in 1815 for £362, and rediscovered in 1900, by Sir Claude Phillips, hung high up in the bathroom), Netscher's *The Lace Maker* (Gallery XIII, No. 206), Rembrandt's *The Good Samaritan* (Gallery XIII, No. 203) and the *Landscape with a Coach* (Gallery XIV, No. 229 ; bought in 1823 for 350 guineas), and Reynolds' *St. John in the Wilderness* (Gallery XVI, No. 48 ; purchased in 1813 for £176 8s.). The third Marquess also bought Terborch's *The Peace of Munster*, given many years later by Sir Richard Wallace to the National Gallery, and he received Gainsborough's *Perdita* (Gallery XVI, No. 42) as a present from the Prince Regent to whom he bequeathed Van Dyck's *The Artist as the Shepherd Paris* (Gallery XVI, No. 85). The last-named picture owes its place in the Collection to-day to the fact that the King died before the Marquess.

The third Marquess of Hertford died on 1st March 1842 at Old Dorchester House, where he had, to quote Harriette Wilson, " a vast collection of gold and silver coins, portraits, drawings, curious snuff-boxes and watches." He was succeeded by his elder son Richard (1800–1870).

LORD HENRY SEYMOUR

A younger son, Lord Henry Seymour (1805–1859) inherited his mother's large fortune. He lived mostly in France, rarely visited England, and cut an eccentric figure in Paris, where he was known as *Milord Arsouille*. In the Carnivals of 1834–35 he attempted to introduce the Italian custom of throwing comfits and coins among the

crowd. He is said also to have been one of the pro-
moters of the *can-can*. A prominent figure of the racing
world, Lord Henry founded the Jockey Club, was one of
the eighteen originators of a society for the encourage-
ment of horse-breeding in France, and even bequeathed
money for the support of four favourite horses, which
were never again to be saddled. He died in Paris (where
he was born), and was buried in his mother's vault at
Père-Lachaise.

THE FOURTH MARQUESS

The fourth Marquess was the leading spirit in the formation of the Collection. His early activities in the army,
in diplomacy (at the embassies in Paris and in Constanti-
nople), and in politics (as Member for County Antrim until
1828) never caught his whole-hearted interest, and after
achieving distinction in the House of Commons, where he
won the praise of Peel, who saw in him a future Prime
Minister, he withdrew from public life and, on his succession, lived in Paris as an art-collecting recluse. Like
many men to whom the arts are a passion, the fourth
Marquess was eccentric, being often stimulated to a
great decision by some contrastingly trifling incident.
It is said, indeed, that the final factor which induced him
to leave London for Paris was a dispute with the civic
authorities over the drainage of one of his London houses.

In Paris the fourth Marquess went little into society,
except for occasional visits to the Jockey Club and more
frequent games of whist with the celebrated players
known as *La Grosse Partie* at the *Union*, the meeting-place
of French aristocracy. In full accordance with the Hertford tradition of keeping up several houses at the same
time, the fourth Marquess became possessed of three
properties in Paris in addition to his London houses,
Old Dorchester House, two houses in Piccadilly, Manchester House and No. 13 Berkeley Square, not to

mention his estates in Suffolk and Ireland. His first collection was made at Bagatelle, the small summer pavilion (known, sometimes, as *Folie d'Artois*) in the Bois de Boulogne, which had been built in 1777 by François-Joseph Belanger (1744–1818) for the Comte d'Artois, later Charles X, who desired it for the entertainment of his sister-in-law, Queen Marie-Antoinette. It was said to have been built in one month. Here the Marquess tried to recapture the spirit of the Rococo by seeking out choice furniture and works of art of the eighteenth century and by decorating the park laid out by Blaikeley, an expert landscape-gardener, with fine pieces of sculpture. It was in these grounds, indeed, that the Marquess surprised two of his friends, when they had asked for leave to fight a duel there, by replying that he was not concerned with the risk to their lives, but with the more distressing probability of their faulty marksmanship among his marbles.

The Marquess was fortunate in securing Bagatelle in 1835—before his succession—when it was alienated from the Crown properties. The price paid was three hundred thousand francs. It is said that Louis-Philippe refused to live in it for fear of stepping into Charles' shoes.

Among the few visitors to the Marquess of Hertford at Bagatelle was Napoleon III ; and a summer-house still exists where the Emperor used to watch the little Prince Imperial taking his riding-lessons on a special ground made by the Marquess. This riding-ground was later converted into a rose-garden, many of the roses having been brought from Kew. Every year a rose show takes place, at which representatives of many countries compete for prizes. The house and park were purchased by the City of Paris from the late Sir John Murray Scott in 1904 and are now open to the public.

As well as Bagatelle, Lord Hertford possessed two other houses in Paris ; one which he used himself, 2 rue

Laffitte, at the corner where the street joins the Boulevard des Italiens, and another, close by, for the use of his brother, Lord Henry Seymour, and his mother, 1 (afterwards 3) rue Taitbout. In both these residences the Collection accumulated, and after the death of Lord Henry in 1859, the fine contents of the house in the rue Taitbout were merged with the treasures in the rue Laffitte. Lord Hertford's Paris house no longer stands, and the famous " rotunda " at the angle of the street is replaced by a *bureau-de-change*.* The rooms were apparently packed with pictures, furniture, sculpture, porcelain, books and bibelots of all kinds. One storey was set apart as a *garde-meuble*, to contain all the spare furniture which Lord Hertford accumulated. In one of the rooms a kind of stage was erected to accommodate a collection of clocks. About 250 pictures hung in the gallery and rooms on the first floor alone. The French pictures were here, and a considerable number of the other schools. At the far end, on the Boulevard side, was the Marquess' bedroom, which contained a Reynolds, perhaps the *Mrs. Robinson* (now in Gallery IX, No. 45 ; bought by Mawson in 1859 for £840), Greuze's *Sophie Arnould* (in Gallery XVIII, No. 403 ; purchased in 1858 for 5,600 francs) and over 200 miniatures. In the rotunda were hung the Marquess' favourite paintings, notably the four panels by Boucher (in Gallery XIX, Nos. 429, 432, 438, 444 †), *The Laughing Cavalier* (bought in 1865 for 51,000 francs), Rubens' *Isabella Brant* (purchased in 1853 for 18,200 francs), Fragonard's *The Swing* (bought in 1865 for 30,200 francs), and many French pictures of the eighteenth century. A further selection of paintings, rather foreign to our present tastes, included the large group by Gonzales Coques (in Gallery XVI, No. 92 ;

* A building very similar to Lord Hertford's former house stands on the opposite side of the boulevard, at the corner of the rue de Grammont.
† These pictures were bought by Lord Hertford for 10,600 francs in 1851 ; they were then fixed to a screen with a pastoral composition by Lancret at the back of each.

bought by Lord Hertford in 1857 for 45,000 francs, in com-
petition with the Louvre authorities), a *Madonna* by Murillo,
a *Landscape with Cattle* by Paul Potter (Gallery II, No.
189), and pictures by Prud'hon, Decamps and Delaroche.

The passion for collecting gradually outran every
other interest in which the fourth Marquess had ever
indulged. He opened his house only to a few intimate
friends, and tried to beguile the sufferings of ill-health by
interviewing dealers, who brought their objects to him
at his house so as to save him the strain of appearing in
the sale-rooms. His yearly income of over two hundred
thousand pounds enabled him to purchase works of art
at unheard-of prices (which to-day seem moderate
enough) and his name became famous in Paris as that
of the eccentric English *milord* who, from the seclusion
of Bagatelle or the rue Laffitte, challenged all the Crowned
Heads of Europe in their endeavours to beautify their
palaces with unique masterpieces of art.

Things were everything to the fourth Marquess, and
to him people meant little. " *Il n'aurait même pas écarté le
rideau de sa fenêtre pour voir une révolution passer dans la rue* "
was a comment by a contemporary. One of his few
devoted companions was his faithful valet John Orme.
The Marquess' sympathy with external life was extended
principally to animals, and at Bagatelle he gave up
certain portions of the grounds as a kind of hospital for
old horses and dogs, which he used constantly to visit,
perhaps out of fellow-feeling, during his last illness.

His respect for art, however, prompted him to sym-
pathize with penurious artists ; and the Goncourts
recount that Lord Hertford, being anxious to make the
acquaintance of Balzac at a time when the novelist could
only go out at night for fear of a writ being served on
him, offered to pay his debts of 50,000 francs or more in
return for a visit. The offer was graciously refused.

Even in London, which the Marquess spasmodically
visited (on such occasions he would usually stay at

No. 13 Berkeley Square), the work of accumulation
went on. The Marquess' English agent, S. M. Mawson,
was instructed to buy works of art for his various seats
in London and the country, as well as to look after the
inherited treasures which were already in these houses.
Sixty letters addressed by the Marquess to Mawson,
between the years 1848 and 1856, were purchased for
the Collection from the latter's daughter in 1912, and
another was the gift of Mr. Fairfax Murray. These illustrate the growth of the London collection and the personal taste of the writer. Mawson, in his work as agent,
had carefully to consider Lord Hertford's expressed
tastes which, besides being concentrated on objects only
of the highest quality, were restricted to certain points of
style and subject. French pictures of the eighteenth
century were the Marquess' predominating passion, and
he did not greatly care for the " Old Masters," with the
exception of Murillo, for whose rich, mellow quality he
expressed an admiration. The Primitives never attracted
him ; their archaism, asceticism and incompleteness
left him dissatisfied. " I only like pleasing pictures," he
wrote to Mawson. " Primitive Masters . . . I have not
yet adopted and I do not think I ever will." " I confess,"
he wrote on another occasion, " I do not much like the
portrait of an old man, however fine it may be ; it is
not pleasing." Certain early nineteenth century painters
attracted him, particularly Bonington ("I like this
Master very much, though he is not much admired in
our country "), Horace Vernet, Decamps, Delaroche
and Meissonier. But, although the Marquess' views were
strong, they were not inflexible, and Mawson, who was
a man of taste with a breadth of vision, guided Lord
Hertford's judgment by advising him to buy pictures by
the great Flemish, Dutch and Spanish Masters, many of
which the Marquess had never seen.

The letters to Mawson give a remarkable insight into
certain aspects of the Marquess' character : notably his

great taste and individual judgment, his astuteness as regards prices (which engendered a strong desire for secrecy in all his purchases) and the confidence which he repeatedly expressed in Mawson's artistic discrimination. Constant references too are made to his own ever-weakening health, his rheumatism, influenza and sleeplessness. In 1855, however, he made a valiant effort to combat physical fatigue by accepting the office of Juror at the Exhibition, where he had to be in his place each morning at nine o'clock. In 1857, he lent forty-four of his pictures to the Art Treasures Exhibition in Manchester, which gave to the English public a slight foretaste of the Collection's wealth. When the absence of these pictures from his collection was referred to, the Marquess replied, " *Au fait, je ne suis pas fâché d'envoyer mes tableaux à Manchester ; ce sera pour moi une occasion de les voir.*"

In August 1870 the Marquess died at Bagatelle. As he had never married, the title and entailed estates passed to the eldest son of his father's cousin, Sir George Seymour, who received the family seat of Ragley Hall, in Warwickshire. But the collection with all unentailed property passed to Richard Wallace, probably his illegitimate son, who knew nothing of his fortune until after the funeral, when the will was discovered in the drawer of a piece of furniture. The Marquess' death occurred during the opening stages of the Franco-Prussian War ; and the funeral procession to the Père-Lachaise took four hours to cross Paris, which was seething with public excitement and military activity.

The English newspapers dismissed the passing of the great collector with little more than a few smug or unflattering references to an unpatriotic eccentric, who had led a life of libertinage in a foreign capital. French writers, however, paid tribute to a highly cultured gentleman, who combined intense shyness with complete courtesy, a witty talker amongst his few intimate friends, a man-of-letters, and a classical scholar of distinction.

SIR RICHARD WALLACE

Richard Wallace (1818–1890) * was born when the fourth Marquess of Hertford was a youth of eighteen. He was known in his earlier years as Richard Jackson, which was the surname of the coachman in whose charge he was placed. The identity of his mother and the full circumstances of his birth and parentage remain a mystery.

Temperamentally, Wallace was the rightful heir to the Hertford treasures, for he inherited to the full the Marquess' passion for collecting. Independently he formed a collection of pictures and works of art which he sold in 1857. Afterwards, as " Monsieur Richard," he helped Lord Hertford in his purchases. Wallace's scheme of adding to the collection filled up gaps in the representation of certain schools. The most serious *lacunæ* were noticeable in the Dutch pictures collected by the third Marquess, and Richard Wallace repaired these omissions as well as branching out in other directions which the third and fourth Marquesses had left unexplored. Unlike the fourth Marquess, Richard Wallace was interested in the art of more distant times, and admired medieval and renaissance works. He purchased the complete collection of medieval *objets d'art* of the Comte de Nieuwerkerke for 400,000 francs, and the best part of Sir Samuel Meyrick's collection of armour for £73,000.

Richard Wallace spent his earlier life in Paris in the company of Bohemian folk, and he later became known in the city for his charity as well as for his artistic tastes. As a result of his public work in Paris during the Franco-Prussian war he was awarded a baronetcy (24th December 1871). During the siege of Paris he organized three ambulance corps, one for the field and two for the city ; subscribed 100,000 francs for the victims of the bombardment and endowed the Hertford British Hospital

---

* A posthumous portrait-bust of Sir Richard Wallace by E. Hannaux, dated 1899, is in the Founders' Room (S 46).

(opened by King Edward VII—as Prince of Wales—in 1879). He also erected in the capital two hundred drinking fountains, for the benefit of people and animals. These fountains, later known as *wallaces*, were designed and executed by Charles-Auguste Lebourg, the sculptor of the busts of the fourth Marquess (S44) and of Lady Wallace (S45), now in the Founders' Room. Many of the fountains were removed in 1931, owing to lack of space.

During the Commune (1871), which transcended the Siege in panic and licence, Richard Wallace, becoming alarmed for the safety of his possessions, brought the greater part of the collection over to London to be installed in Hertford House, much to the chagrin of the Parisians. Many repairs and reconstructions to the dilapidated London House were necessary, and pending the workmen's invasion Richard Wallace lent most of the pictures and other objects of art to the Bethnal Green Museum (1872–75). The exhibition, which was opened by the Prince and Princess of Wales, is said to have been visited by 5,000,000 people. Another part of the Collection, including the Library, was housed in the Pantechnicon, and perished in the fire of 1874 ; yet another portion remained at Bagatelle and another at the rue Laffitte.

Sir Richard Wallace's concern for public enrichment had prompted him, towards the end of his life, to consider the possibilities of a national museum for his treasures, but ill-health, combined with difficulties over the Portman lease of Hertford House, drove the idea temporarily from his mind, and in his will he left everything unconditionally to his wife, Amélie-Julie-Charlotte Castelnau, whom he had married in 1871. There was one son, Georges, born out of wedlock, who had served as a Captain in the Franco-Prussian War and had won the Légion d'Honneur. He died before his father, leaving several children.

Sir Richard's life in England was divided between Manchester Square and Sudbourne Hall, Suffolk, which he bought from the fifth Marquess. Wallace also built a house on the Lisburn Estate, County Antrim, but only once stayed in it, although he was a member for Lisburn from 1873 till 1885. In Suffolk he would entertain large shooting parties, but in London his house was open to guests only on very formal or very intimate occasions. Few but Sir Richard's closest friends entered the house, although at one time certain privileged ticket-holders were admitted to the Collection on specified Wednesdays.

The last four years of Sir Richard's life were spent chiefly in Paris and at Bagatelle, where his habits as an eccentric recluse, inherited from his father, grew upon him. It is said that at Bagatelle he had a sliding panel through which he could watch his guests at table, yet remain unseen by them. He died in Paris on 20th July 1890, and his body was placed, by his request, under Lord Henry Seymour's in the Hertford vault at the Père-Lachaise. Four years later (23rd May 1894) Lady Wallace made a will, which bequeathed his Collection to the British Nation, an act which graciously fulfilled her husband's unachieved desire. The terms of the Bequest insisted that the Collection should be a closed one.

LADY WALLACE

Lady Wallace outlived her husband by seven years. She was buried beside him in the Père-Lachaise, after a preliminary service at St. Thomas's Church, Orchard Street (demolished in March 1932 ; the site is now occupied by an extension of Messrs. Selfridge), where she and Sir Richard used to go on Sunday mornings.

SIR JOHN MURRAY SCOTT

At Lady Wallace's death the link with the founders was not broken. Sir John Murray Scott, Sir Richard's secretary, who had been his companion in Paris through-out the Siege and Commune, and who became the con-fidential adviser to Lady Wallace after her husband's death, became residuary legatee of Hertford House. He received possession of the Lisburn Estate, of the remainder of the lease of Hertford House and of everything there not placed on its ground and first floors, of the house in the rue Laffitte, the pavilion of Bagatelle, and of all the art treasures in the last two houses. After his death the pictures and objects of art in his London house, 5, Connaught Place, originally part of Sir Richard Wallace's Collection, were sold at Christies' (June 1913) ; he had sold Bagatelle in 1904, and Houdon's *Baigneuse* which was there (it is now in the Altman Collection, Metropolitan Museum, New York). The contents of the Paris house, with the exception of a copy of Watteau's *L'Accord Parfait* and four battle-pieces by Horace Vernet, left to the National Gallery, he bequeathed to Lady Sackville. This bequest was unsuccessfully contested at law by Sir John Murray Scott's sisters. Lady Sackville, in 1914, disposed of the greater part of her legacy to Messrs. Jacques Seligmann et fils, Paris. Many of the finest works of art went to America ; and among the most important former possessions of Lord Hertford and Sir Richard Wallace, now dispersed, may be mentioned busts by Houdon of *Cagliostro* and *Sophie Arnould*, now in America, a bronze version of Houdon's *La Frileuse*, *Les Œufs Cassés* by Greuze, now in the Metropolitan Museum, New York, a silver and enamelled chandelier by Gouthière, a note-book with miniatures which belonged to Marie-Antoinette, now in the Veil-Picard Collection, Paris, and a diamond necklace which had belonged to Catherine Parr. Sculptures by Clodion, pictures by Boilly, much splendid furniture, many tapestries, coloured prints, and a superb collection of French books of the 18th century (bought in 1914 by Messrs. Bumpus), went besides.

Until his death Sir John was closely concerned with the fitting-up of the Collection as a national museum. For his services he had been created a baronet and was one of the original Trustees of the Collection. It was

3

during a visit to Manchester Square on the 17th January 1912, made for the purpose of furnishing information on the history of the Collection, that he died of an attack of apoplexy in the old Board Room, now known as the Founders' Room. Thus, in the appropriate surroundings of Hertford House, the final chapter in the Hertford-Wallace history was brought to a sudden close.

HERTFORD HOUSE

The existence of Hertford House in Manchester Square is due to an unexpected turn of history. In the last years of the reign of Queen Anne, elaborate preparations were made to lay out a square named after the Queen with a church in the middle. But the Queen's death frustrated the project, and part of the square was bought by the Duke of Manchester, who built his house—called Manchester House—in a plot of land on the north side, where good duck-shooting was obtainable. At the Duke's death, the house passed from ducal to ambassadorial residents, and Manchester House became the Spanish Embassy, with its chapel near by, now the well-known Roman Catholic Church, St. James's, Spanish Place.* Later it is said that the French Embassy took up its residence there, and that Talleyrand and Guizot were among its occupants. The circumstances of the transference of the house to the Hertford family are uncertain, but the transaction had occurred by the time of the second Marquess. The fourth Marquess, although he had part of his Collection in the house, spent little time there, and it was not until Sir Richard Wallace brought over from France the greater part of his father's Collection, in 1872, that Manchester House fulfilled again its proper function as a stately residence. Then great alterations were made ; picture galleries (now No. XVI and side galleries) were built over the garden at the back, and stabling, coach-

* The church was removed in recent years to George Street, when the flats were built in Spanish Place.

houses and an elaborately tiled smoking-room (now Gallery IV) were arranged below. In the basement the cobble-stones of the old stable-yard can still be seen. In a grant of a coat-of-arms, dated June 1871, Sir Richard's London address was given as Hertford House, which shows that he paid this tribute to the great collector almost immediately upon coming into the property, an act of courtesy paralleled by his naming the Hertford British Hospital after the fourth Marquess rather than after himself.

It was not Sir Richard's or Lady Wallace's intention that the Collection, when given to the nation, should necessarily remain at Hertford House, and a condition of the will was that the Government should agree to give a site in a central part of London and build thereon a special museum to contain the Collection. Later, various suggestions were made, including one that new buildings to house the Collection should be erected near the National Gallery, where Messrs. Hampton's now stands ; but the Committee, headed by Lord Lansdowne, finally decided that for reasons of economy the Collection should remain in its present home. To adapt Hertford House to the demands of a museum, several changes were necessary. The stables and coach-houses were converted into Galleries (V–VIII), a mezzanine-floor, of which some blocked-up windows may still be seen on the east side of the present building, was abolished, and the first-floor living-rooms were altered to admit the public.* In June 1900 the Collection was opened as a national museum by Edward VII, then Prince of Wales.

The mansion's history did not remain undisturbed. Seventeen years after its opening as a national museum

* Some of Sir Richard Wallace's old servants were retained. A brick in the wall beside the western of the two front gateways bears the initials *A.P.* and the date *1897*, this mark being that of Augustus Piolaine, an old and trusted servant who, fearing dismissal on Lady Wallace's death, left this memento of his service. Another curious connexion with the domestic life at Hertford House is a set of copper kitchen utensils, marked with Sir Richard Wallace's crest, now in the possession of Mr. Vanderbeeken at his cookery establishment, "Below Stairs," No. 17 Berkeley Square.

the Great War necessitated its closing and complete dis-
mantling. From 1914 onwards its principal treasures were
gradually committed to the basements, but in 1917, when
air-raids became increasingly serious, the entire Collection
was removed to the new Post Office Tube at Paddington
Station. The house, however, did not remain untenanted,
and the marquesses, ambassadors and great collectors
of the past were followed by officials of the Geographical
Section of the Admiralty Intelligence Division. Later
further changes were made, and the Naval staff gave way
to the Accounts Branch of the Ministry of Munitions.
But this unexpected tenantry was only a strange interlude
between two periods of calm. After the Armistice the
house was gradually cleared of its new occupants and
further redecoration rapidly ensued. By the autumn of
1920 the works of art were freed from their subterranean
imprisonment, and in November of the same year the
public was again admitted to the treasures of Hertford
House. Since then, three new galleries have been built
on the second floor, and the walls of the principal suites
of rooms have been hung with silk, the gift of Lord
Duveen. These include the old state drawing-room (now
Gallery II) which was formerly panelled and gilded by
Sir Richard Wallace in the taste of his time. The
Founders have placed upon their successors the obligation
of maintaining, in a worthy manner, the finest gift of its
kind ever bequeathed by a single individual to the State.

INDEX

St. Dunstan's-in-the-West, Fleet Street, 6

St. James's Church, Spanish Place, 18

St. John in the Wilderness, 7

St. Thomas's Church, Orchard Street, 16

Scott, Sir John Murray, 9, 16, 17, 18

Seligmann et fils, Messrs., 17

Selwyn of Matson, George, 5

Seymour, Algernon. *See* Somerset, seventh Duke of

Seymour, Edward. *See* Hertford, first Earl of

Seymour, Lord Henry, 7, 8, 10, 16,

Seymour, Sir George, 13

Seymour-Conway, Francis. *See* Hertford, first Marquess of

Seymour - Conway, Francis Charles. *See* Hertford, third Marquess of

Seymour-Conway, Francis Ingram. *See* Hertford, second Marquess of

Seymour-Conway, the Ladies Elizabeth and Frances, 2

Seymour-Conway, Richard. *See* Hertford, fourth Marquess of

Somerset, first Duke of. *See* Hertford, first Earl of

Somerset, seventh Duke of, 1

Sophie Arnould, 10, 17

Stanhope, Anne, 1

Steyne, Marquess of, 4

Sudbourne Hall, Suffolk, 15

Swing, The, 10

Taitbout, rue, No. 1...10

Talleyrand, Charles-Maurice de 4, 18

Terborch, Gerard, 7

Thackeray, William Makepeace, 4

Vanderbeeken, Mr., 19

Vanity Fair, 4

Veil-Picard Collection, 17

Vernet, Horace, 12

Veronese, Paul, 7

Vision of St. Catherine, 6

Wallace, Captain Georges, 15

Wallace, Lady, 15, 16, 19

Wallace, Sir Richard, xii, 7, 13, 14, 15, 16, 17, 18, 19

Walpole, Horace, 5

Walpole, Sir Robert, 2

War-time, Collection in, 19, 20

Watteau, Antoine, 17

Wilson, Harriette, 5, 7

PRINTED IN GREAT BRITAIN BY WILLIAM CLOWES AND SONS, LTD., LONDON AND BECCLES.

PLATES

(I) PERSONS, PLACES AND OBJECTS CONNECTED WITH THE HISTORY OF THE COLLECTION

(b) THE SECOND MARQUESS OF HERTFORD WHEN
VISCOUNT BEAUCHAMP
Engraving by G. S. Shury, after a painting by
Sir J. Reynolds

(a) THE FIRST MARQUESS OF HERTFORD
Engraving by J. Watts, after a painting by Sir J. Reynolds
at Ragley Hall, Alcester

PLATE II

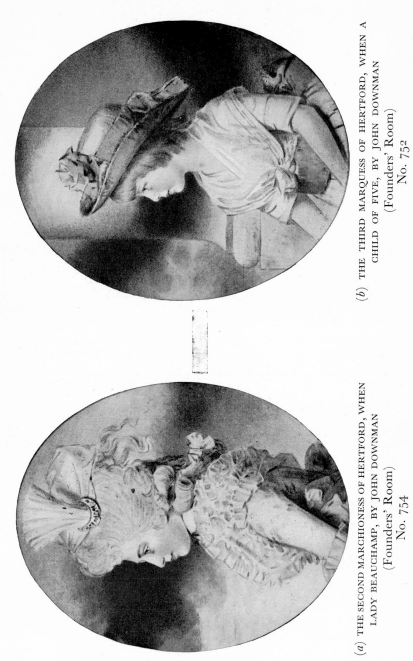

(a) THE SECOND MARCHIONESS OF HERTFORD, WHEN
LADY BEAUCHAMP, BY JOHN DOWNMAN
(Founders' Room)
No. 754

(b) THE THIRD MARQUESS OF HERTFORD, WHEN A
CHILD OF FIVE, BY JOHN DOWNMAN
(Founders' Room)
No. 752

PLATE III

(c) MARIA FAGNANI, THIRD MARCHIONESS OF HERTFORD, BY RICHARD COSWAY

(b) A CARICATURE BY R. DIGHTON OF THE THIRD MARQUESS WHEN EARL OF YARMOUTH, 1818

(a) THE THIRD MARQUESS OF HERTFORD
From a painting by Sir T. Lawrence, formerly at St. Dunstan's

PLATE IV

(*a*) THE AUTOMATON CLOCK AS RE-ERECTED ON
ST. DUNSTAN'S-IN-THE-WEST, FLEET STREET

(*b*) ST. DUNSTAN'S LODGE, REGENT'S PARK

(NOTE.—The rectangular space on the left-hand building is where
the automaton clock formerly stood.)

PLATE V

(*a*) THE FOURTH MARQUESS OF HERTFORD
From a photograph

(*b*) THE HOUSE OF THE FOURTH MARQUESS IN THE RUE
LAFFITTE, SHOWING THE ROTUNDA

PLATE VI

A VIEW OF THE BOULEVARD DES ITALIENS, *c.* 1860

On the right is the domed house of the fourth Marquess at the corner of the rue Laffitte and, beyond, that of Lord Henry Seymour at the near corner of the rue Taitbout

PLATE VII

SIR RICHARD WALLACE

From the photography by J. Thomson, 1888.

PLATE VIII

(*a*) A SHOOTING PARTY AT SUDBOURNE HALL, SUFFOLK

SIR JOHN MURRAY SCOTT IS ON THE EXTREME RIGHT. THE SPOT IS IDENTIFIABLE
AS THE PATHWAY TO NEWTON. ORFORD CASTLE IS ON THE HORIZON ON
THE RIGHT.

From a painting by Alfred Decaen in Orford Town Hall

(*b*) A SHOOTING PARTY AT SUDBOURNE HALL, SUFFOLK

IN THE CENTRE IS SEATED MR. DISNEY, MAYOR OF ORFORD. LADY WALLACE
IS STEPPING OUT OF THE CARRIAGE ASSISTED BY CAPTAIN WALLACE.
ON THE EXTREME LEFT IS THE RECTOR OF CHILSFORD. SIR RICHARD
WALLACE IS SEATED AT THE END OF THE TABLE ON THE RIGHT.

From a painting by Alfred Decaen in Orford Town Hall

PLATE IX

(*a*) THE FOURTH MARQUESS OF HERTFORD, LADY WALLACE AND SIR RICHARD
WALLACE AT BAGATELLE

(*b*) BAGATELLE IN THE TIME OF THE FOURTH MARQUESSS

The figures are, possibly, members of the household staff. Among the
statues may be seen a bronze version of Houdon's *La Frileuse*, no
longer in the collection

PLATE X

(*a*) THE BREAKFAST ROOM AT BAGATELLE

(*b*) THE SALON AT BAGATELLE

PLATE XI

(*a*) THE EXTERIOR OF BAGATELLE IN THE TIME OF THE FOURTH MARQUESS

(*b*) BAGATELLE AS IT IS TO-DAY

PLATE XII

(*a*) THE HERTFORD BRITISH HOSPITAL, PARIS

(*b*) A " WALLACE FOUNTAIN " IN THE PLACE SAINT-SULPICE, PARIS

(*c*) THE HERTFORD-WALLACE TOMB IN THE CEMETERY OF PÈRE-LACHAISE, PARIS

PLATE XIII

(*a*) MANCHESTER (HERTFORD) HOUSE IN 1813

(*b*) HERTFORD HOUSE TO-DAY

(II)   HERTFORD   HOUSE

AS   A   PRIVATE   RESIDENCE

FROM   PHOTOGRAPHS   MADE   BY

MR.   J.   J.   THOMSON   ABOUT   1897

PLATE XIV

(*a*) THE COURTYARD OF HERTFORD HOUSE

(*b*) ENTRANCE HALL AND GRAND STAIRCASE OF HERTFORD HOUSE

PLATE XV

BACK STATE ROOM
(Now Gallery II)

PLATE XVI

SIXTEENTH-CENTURY ROOM, LOOKING NORTH

(Now Gallery III, back)

PLATE XVII

SIXTEENTH-CENTURY ROOM, LOOKING SOUTH, INTO CANALETTO ROOM

(Now Gallery III, back)

PLATE XVIII

THE BREAKFAST ROOM OR SMALL DINING ROOM

(Now Gallery IX)

PLATE XIX

THE BILLIARD ROOM

(Now Gallery X)

PLATE XX

THE DINING ROOM

(Now Gallery XI)

PLATE XXI

PLATE XXII

THE " REYNOLDS " ROOM, LOOKING EAST

(Now Gallery XII, front)

PLATE XXIII

THE LONG DRAWING ROOM, LOOKING SOUTH-WEST

(Now Gallery XII, back)

PLATE XXIV

THE EAST DRAWING ROOM, LOOKING NORTH

(Now Gallery XIII)

PLATE XXV

THE ORIENTAL ARMOURY, LOOKING NORTH
(Now Gallery XIV)

PLATE XXVI

THE " MODERN " GALLERY, LOOKING NORTH

(Now Gallery XV)

PLATE XXVII

THE "MODERN GALLERY," LOOKING SOUTH
(Now Gallery XV)

PLATE XXVIII

THE " MODERN " GALLERY, PART OF THE EAST WALL

(Now Gallery XV)

PLATE XXIX

THE LONG PICTURE GALLERY, LOOKING WEST

(Now Gallery XVI)

PLATE XXX

THE LONG PICTURE GALLERY, LOOKING EAST

(Now Gallery XVI)

NOTE.—The vase in the foreground is a pair to the vase (S 32) by Clodion, now in Gallery XXI. It is no longer in the Collection.

PLATE XXXI

THE LONG PICTURE GALLERY, NORTH WALL, EAST (I)
(Now Gallery XVI)

PLATE XXXII

THE LONG PICTURE GALLERY, NORTH WALL, EAST (2)
(Now Gallery XVI)

PLATE XXXIII

THE LONG PICTURE GALLERY, NORTH WALL, EAST (3)
(Now Gallery XVI)

PLATE XXXIV

THE LONG PICTURE GALLERY, NORTH WALL, EAST (4)
(Now Gallery XVI)

PLATE XXXV

THE LONG PICTURE GALLERY, NORTH WALL, CENTRE
(Now Gallery XVI)

PLATE XXXVI

THE LONG PICTURE GALLERY, NORTH WALL, WEST (I)
(Now Gallery XVI)

PLATE XXXVII

THE LONG PICTURE GALLERY, NORTH WALL, WEST (2)
(Now Gallery XVI)

PLATE XXXVIII

THE LONG PICTURE GALLERY, WEST WALL

(Now Gallery XVI)

PLATE XXXIX

THE LONG PICTURE GALLERY, SOUTH WALL, CENTRE
(Now Gallery XVI)

PLATE XL

THE LONG PICTURE GALLERY, SOUTH WALL, EAST (I)
(Now Gallery XVI)

PLATE XLI

THE LONG PICTURE GALLERY, SOUTH WALL, EAST (2)
(Now Gallery XVI)

PLATE XLII

THE SOUTH-EAST CORNER OF THE LONG PICTURE GALLERY
(Now Gallery XVI)

PLATE XLIII

THE LONG PICTURE GALLERY, EAST WALL

(Now Gallery XVI)

PLATE XLIV

THE EUROPEAN ARMOURY, SOUTH AND EAST WALLS
(Now Gallery XVII)

PLATE XLV

THE EUROPEAN ARMOURY, SOUTH AND WEST WALLS
(Now Gallery XVII)

PLATE XLVI

THE EUROPEAN ARMOURY, NORTH AND EAST WALLS

(Now Gallery XVII)

PLATE XLVII

THE EUROPEAN ARMOURY, NORTH AND WEST WALLS
(Now Gallery XVII)

PLATE XLVIII

SIR RICHARD WALLACE'S STUDY, EAST AND SOUTH WALLS

(Now Gallery XXI)

PLATE XLIX

MINIATURES IN THE OVAL DRAWING ROOM

(Now Gallery XXII)

PLATE L

MINIATURES IN THE OVAL DRAWING ROOM
(Now Gallery XXII)